The Savior/Shadow

Principle: A Self-Help

Technique

and Philosophy

Using Archetypes

QUILLKEEPERS PRESS

ISBN:979-8-9891531-9-0

Published by Quillkeepers Press, LLC
PO Box 10236
Casa Grande, AZ 85130

This book is dedicated to my father, David.

With his support and encouragement, I was

able to find the courage to write this book.

Thanks Dad!

"And you shall know the truth, and the truth

shall make you free"

—John 8:32 (NKJV)

Chapter I:

Introduction

The book you are now reading is the culmination of years of research, self-discovery, pain, anguish, and life experience. Through this arduous and informative journey, I developed a self-help technique and philosophy that helped me improve my life. It is deeply personal, and I feel it is necessary for me to share it with others.

I believe it is important to do so with the knowledge we gain in this life, to help others, and to give our lives additional meaning.

This self-help technique is a mythologically-based imaginative meditation involving the Goddess Hekate (also spelled "Hecate") and the Christian Son of God, Jesus. The original version with the aforementioned deities is shared, in addition to singular versions involving Hekate and Jesus alone. The accompanying life philosophy is based on these stories involving self-compassion and self-honesty.

It was born from my time as a ChristoPagan (also spelled "Christopagan" or "Christo-Pagan"); I will provide an overview so there is a foundational understanding of how these processes—which I have dubbed the Savior/Shadow Principle (SSP), came about. By sharing this, I wish to pass on the knowledge I gained from the SSP and help free those burdened with decisions from their past. I am no longer ChristoPagan, and instead of feeling guilty for going down a seemingly unusual path, I am embracing my past. I am mining my experiences for the "jewels" they offer, i.e., the insights into myself and life in general. From this, I can grow into a stronger human being, in addition to formulating life plans that are more in tune with my actual nature, i.e., through greater self-honesty.

Though I am sharing my spiritual journey, I am in no way suggesting a particular religion or deity for you. A core goal of the SSP is to engage in an honest evaluation of your life. I am sharing the SSP because it allowed me to be honest with myself and make necessary changes for the better. Though I originally had a more spiritual relationship with both deities, I am sharing them now as archetypes: examples of how to tap into helpful feelings and mindset to encourage greater self-honesty. I know that may seem like a lot, but I am confident that once I introduce their stories and the thoughts behind their presence in this technique and philosophy, all will come together nicely.

Finally, I am not a mental health professional but am merely sharing a technique that proved beneficial to me. I will also share ideas from others that support the Savior/Shadow Principle. However, the information discussed should not take the place of mental health care; if you are having problems, please seek out a mental health professional in your area.

Chapter II:

My Personal Story

After several difficult and disappointing years, in addition to a healthy dose of mid-life crisis (see Appendix A)—I left Christianity and embarked upon a journey through alternative religion. I wasn't finding solace in my faith at the time and was searching for something more.

I was also greatly attracted to Wicca and New Age philosophy. I began reading and researching, testing and trying, learning all I could about these alternative practices. Each new discovery truly inspired me.

While I began integrating these new practices into my life, I still felt a pull from Christianity, namely Jesus. At the time, I came to believe that all religions were a cultural interpretation of "Source" energy, or divine creative energy (I will speak more on this later). Though I enjoyed these new practices and found them to be life-changing, I felt a lack of connection to the *deities* or, more precisely, *archetypal energies* that I was reading about and interacting with. It was then that I began integrating more Christian aspects into my religious practice. I discovered more people who practiced a similar lifestyle and found related books as well. Essentially, this is how I became ChristoPagan; a term I learned from these encounters.

I felt a greater understanding of self through my new faith. I was learning and growing at a rapid pace. I was more self-aware and honest with myself than ever before. I allowed myself to go down different rabbit-holes of interest, unbarred by thinking something wasn't what a "good person" *should* be reading. I learned about Tarot, Astrology, and Magick.

During this time of exploration, I stumbled upon the writings of Carl G. Jung. I was mesmerized! I felt ideas I had—but couldn't fully articulate, were being written about in great detail and extended to areas I couldn't even imagine. I was very interested in the psychologization of religion, though I wasn't familiar with the terminology to be able to share my thoughts with anyone legitimately. For example, I noticed how the Serenity Prayer was helpful to people to let go of the past (by "giving to God" the negative feelings of things that could not be changed), accept one's circumstances, and be motivated to change or act in such a way that would help them improve their situations (McAfee, "Not Just a Necklace"). I noticed how spells, often described as a type of "focused prayer" among practitioners, had a soothing psychological component; one could feel that they had done everything they could in a situation, that they were giving their issue to their deity of choice, the Universe, etc. Thus, removing negative feelings and being able to move forward with less emotional stress.

My ChristoPagan path was Eclectic Wicca-inspired, but this is not necessarily true for others who identify with that label. I worked with a patron god and goddess ("matron goddess" was the terminology I ascribed to at that point of my spiritual journey, though the appropriate term to use would have been "patron goddess." I have cited works I wrote at that time, so the erroneous wording will be apparent if you look up those papers (rough drafts!). However, in this work, I will exclusively use the correct "patron" to describe both god and goddess. There's nothing wrong with admitting mistakes; we are always learning and growing!). I primarily worshipped these deities, though I would work with others at times depending upon their background, like petitioning Aphrodite for assistance with matters of the heart. Because I believed in Source, I didn't think I was working with different deities or hard polytheism. Rather, I felt I was working with various aspects of Source energy or archetypes, referred to as soft polytheism. I also believed a spell was like a focused prayer and that petitioning specific energy allowed for purity, a zeroing in upon my issue.

As far as patron deities in Eclectic Wicca (meaning individualized Wicca, in traditional Wicca, the practices are more formalized), they can be those you have an affinity for. I felt a natural draw to Jesus; he perfectly exemplified the male divine creative energy to me. As far as a patron goddess, that took me a bit longer, but I did find myself drawn to the Goddess Hekate. Hekate is associated with "scary" things like witchcraft, for example. But she was also associated with positive things and depicted as a more all-encompassing-type deity in the Chaldean Oracles (more on this later)..... I also really loved hearing of her kindness in the story of Persephone, Demeter, and Hades, at least in the version I heard. I will share this in a later chapter; as a sidenote, there are different versions, but I will discuss only one. I found her to be a complex and misunderstood deity that resonated with me. It was my ChristoPagan path, my interactions with my patron deities, in addition to researching and learning more about them, that inspired me to create the Savior/Shadow Principle; a meditative self-help technique and life philosophy inspired by the stories of both Jesus and Hekate.

I would like to add that my experience is anecdotal and not meant to be the end-all on ChristoPagans, Wiccans, Pagans in general, etc. I can only share my experiences. There are many ChristoPagans who practice very differently and would define the path unlike I would. As far as ChristoPaganism, it is controversial; it can be viewed as heretical by Christians and even by Pagans. Also, some contention surrounds eclectic and traditional forms of Wicca. All of this is outside the scope of this text. But again, I can only share how I practiced and my personal experiences.

My Current Path

I later returned to Christianity, though I am a bit non-traditional. While I enjoyed my time as a ChristoPagan, I felt drawn back to being a Christian. I often found myself thinking about grace and felt my former faith was closer to my ideals; my exploration into alternative religion, self-honesty, and the growth from both led me to those realizations (see Appendix B).

I share this to show how the Savior/Shadow Principle changed as I changed: there are ChristoPagan, Pagan, and Christianfriendly versions. I know my path was not very traditional, but each step was what I needed at the time. Even though I have returned to my former faith, I am not ashamed of the road I have taken to get where I presently am. As far as being Christian, I don't know where on the spectrum I belong. Meaning, what denomination I am best suited for, and I am still seeking, still growing. I am a seeker in general. I won't lose that part of myself because I have now accepted it versus repressing it as I had before my journey into alternative spirituality. Maybe I will be a "sect of one" like Thomas Jefferson famously referred to himself as. I don't know, but I am open to wherever the road leads me.

In the spirit of honesty, I will say that I am not a literalist. I believe when we look at myth and religion literally, there is a richness we lose. We can lose the allegorical blueprint given, in addition to losing our power as well. We can give our issues up to the divine without recognizing the action(s) we must take to better our lives. In this case, I am referring to an overreliance on God; for example, praying to God for assistance in meeting new friends, but not changing your routine, where you go, etc., to meet new people. I have personally done this in the past, and I have seen others do it as well. I'm not saying God isn't real, not at all. I pray. I enjoy reading the Bible. I don't ascribe to literalist's interpretation of scripture. In my opinion, there are similarities in ancient myths that cannot be denied (e.g., Joseph Campbell's "Hero's Journey"); I view the Bible as a collection of real events coupled with allegory. However, I'm not an atheist and believe in the mystery of faith. I don't have all the answers, but I don't need to figure everything out. I believe God is more significant than any one of us can comprehend, and I am open to mystery (I would also add Jesus to that statement; I also revere Mother Mary). I'm just not a literalist, though I have no problem with those who are.

I believe we must find the path that works best for us as individuals. I must be honest with myself about what works for me and encourage you to do the same. That's the overall aim of this book: self-honesty. That way, you can pinpoint what you want in life and make the necessary changes to bring those goals to fruition.

I think with the increased popularity of alternative spirituality and Paganism in the past few years, the Savior/Shadow Principle—whether in its original form or purely Pagan form (these and the Christian version are introduced in later chapters) could be beneficial to others, not just directly, but as a way to gain greater understanding of self by evaluating why one was attracted to certain things at certain times. For instance, it is a common occurrence for people to turn to art after encountering difficulties in life. We all know that the midlife crisis is a period of change: some people end or begin relationships, some revive dreams from the past, some try different spiritual paths, and the list is endless. As for myself, I was highly attracted to worshipping a female deity, as I desired to get more in touch with my feminine energy; I felt that having a patron goddess was balanced and made sense with the natural world. Reflecting on these different periods, I can now see how everything came into my life when I needed it for my spiritual and personal growth journeys.

My path took many twists and turns. I am thankful and believe each of them facilitated my growth and allowed me to be a whole human being. I can look at myself with greater kindness and objectivity due to the SSP, and if it worked for me, it could potentially help others.

Though my religious experiences inspired me, I would like to reiterate that this book is not meant to proselytize. I am not endorsing any religion over another, or religion period. I am only sharing my experiences and train of thought regarding them. Of course, this technique is pliable to suit personal needs. I believe very strongly that each individual needs to choose what is best for their lives, which will allow them to grow into healthy adults who contribute positively to society. If you are not living in accordance with your beliefs, it can breed negativity within yourself, which can spread among those around you. Looking at yourself objectively and being self-honest with what you discover can get you to a more positive place. Not just for yourself but potentially others, by example. We can make positive marks on the world around us by improving ourselves.

Also, you will see me refer to Hekate and Jesus as deities. I do this because they are worshipped as such to this day; I want to respect the beliefs of anyone reading this book. You will also see me refer to the Persephone "myth" and Greek "mythology." This is how these subjects are commonly referenced, so I am merely continuing with that language. Myth and mythology can have several different meanings. For example,

> most Pagans and many others, social scientists among them, use the word "mythology" to mean that grouping of concepts about how the world works that underlies a society or faith

tradition (Higginbotham and Higginbotham 13).

As I said previously, I celebrate your ability to find what works best for you.

Since we have now had an overall introduction to me, my thoughts and motivations, my spiritual path, etc., I think it is now appropriate to dig deeper into ChristoPaganism. It is a lesser-known path, so some discussion is warranted. This information is foundational to the SSP.

Chapter III:

ChristoPaganism:

The Path to this Technique and Philosophy

The Savior/Shadow Principle was born from my time as a ChristoPagan. For those unfamiliar with this spiritual path, my personal definition of it is a melding of Christian and Pagan beliefs, with the ratio of that mix being up to the individual practitioner. Here is some additional information on my thoughts on ChristoPaganism while I was a practitioner:

> Christo-Paganism is a spiritual practice which combines Christian and Pagan beliefs. There is no explicit dogma for Christo-Pagans to follow, which is unlike the various Christian denominations. However, this is similar to the spiritual practice of many solitary or eclectic Wiccans and other Contemporary Pagans. To what degree the combination of the Christian and Pagan beliefs manifest is up to the individual practitioner. For example, some Christo-Pagans work explicitly with the Christian pantheon, while others work with Deities from

other pantheons, in addition to the Christian Deities. Some attend church, while others prefer to be solitary practitioners. Christo-Paganism is an alternative spiritual path filled with personal choice; there is a wide variance as to how those who self-identify in this way practice (McAfee, "Additional Thoughts").

While this is a good summary of my thoughts at the time, I believe it is important that I give an overview of ChristoPaganism from other sources, in addition to a description of my past journey. Again, this is not an endorsement of this religion or any other, but I believe it is important to discuss it to gain understanding. A barrier I have found in talking about the SSP is the seemingly unusual pairing of these two deities or archetypes; I believe it is necessary to share this background information to get to the self-help portion of the SSP.

In the book *ChristoPaganism: An Inclusive Path* by Joyce and River Higginbotham, they offer three different definitions for ChristoPaganism:

1. A spirituality that combines beliefs and practices of Christianity with beliefs and practices of Paganism, or that observes them in parallel.

2. A blended eclectic spiritual tradition involving magickal or earth-centered religions and orthodox or non-orthodox Christianity.

3. An example of an interspiritual or multifaith religious tradition

(Higginbotham and Higginbotham
n. pag.).

As you can see, while my explanation has
some similarities, there isn't one clear-cut
definition.

There are also two interesting and helpful
concepts—among others—the Higginbothams
introduce in their text: that ChristoPaganism is a
practice that is ""post-industrial" or
"aperspectival"" and a form of "interspirituality;"
the former describes "the ability to hold multiple
perspectives at once in an honoring way that does
not need to choose one over the other, or to resolve
seeming contradictions between them," the latter
"encompasses interfaith dialogue, a sharing of
traditions, and the blending of traditions and their
practices" (Higgonbotham & Higgonbotham XV–
XVI, 4). These definitions make perfect sense, as

religion changes throughout time; it is a normal evolution. With current technology, the world has gotten "smaller"—there is access to limitless data at our fingertips via our cellphones. It is only natural that spiritual practices would change, as some would be inspired to find information, communities, etc., that feel more inclusive to them and their ideals. This describes me and my time as a ChristoPagan to a T!

Furthermore, we have examples of these changes throughout history. One of the most obvious is the widely known similarities between the ancient Greek and Roman pantheons; the Romans adapted their pantheon and religious ideals after the Greek model. It is logical that positively received ideas would influence changes. We can also see the development of Christianity throughout time and how it was influenced by cultural changes (and vice versa), for example. I can even recognize changes in Christianity and the Church from when I was younger to the present!

Since we now have a broader understanding of ChristoPaganism, I would like to share more on how I had practiced this alternative spiritual path. As we discussed earlier, I believed in Source, although my patron god and goddess were Jesus and Hekate. They represented very specific energies to me, which would influence my later creation of the SSP. The information below examines my thoughts of both these figures at the time, though deeper explanations will come in the following chapters:

Hecate: Truth (which can be painful), Wisdom (actual and experiential), Tough Love...

Jesus: Humility, Unconditional Love, Quiet Strength (McAfee, "Additional Thoughts").

This chapter serves not only as an introduction to ChristoPaganism but also as a reflection of my personal practice at the time. I learned so much about mythology, philosophy, the world around me, and myself; a fulfilling journey indeed! There are a few concepts that really stand out from this point in my spiritual journey that will assist in explaining the SSP. We will now discuss a few of them.

Chapter IV:

Duality

A concept I further appreciated from studying religions, philosophy, and mythology was duality. Carl G. Jung spoke of the anima; a man's unconscious feminine, and animus; a woman's unconscious masculine. Friedrich Nietzsche, the Apollonian, and the Dionysian; essentially order and chaos, respectively. In

Wicca, there is a balance of deities: the Horned God (not the Devil, but representing nature and a more masculine, virile energy) and the Moon Goddess (the mysterious, receptive feminine energy). In Taoism, the yin and yang represent the balance between interconnected opposites. This duality also extends to self, i.e., our conscious selves and the unconscious part of us, where our shadow resides.

The shadow, or dark, can be a bit difficult to understand (I will use these terms interchangeably). Initially, it can seem to be viewed as "bad," but it represents a variety of concepts. It is the unconscious that is hidden, i.e., the "mysterious" parts of us. It is representative of the feminine. It can be the anima or the outward self, depending upon biological sex (this is per the classic definitions, as feminine being receptive energies, masculine being assertive energies, etc. These are within all of us. This does not include current discussions on gender, which are outside the scope of this text).

The shadow can be frightening. We are afraid of the dark because any number of unknown dangers can be camouflaged by it. It can represent death, not just in the literal sense, but in several ways: egoic death, the "death" or end of a relationship, a transitory phase of life, i.e., growing from childhood to adulthood, etc. Then, there is the negative portion of the feminine. This can be likened to the classically negative traits assigned to Hekate, e.g., witchcraft. However, there are positives with the dark as well.

The shadow can also be likened to the womb: we are each conceived in the dark within our mother's body, then grow to finally travel through the birth canal into the light. It can be likened to the seed that is buried in the dirt, where it grows into a plant that bursts from the earth. While dangers can be hidden in the shadows, it is also where good can be "birthed" from. The mystery that the dark holds can ignite a multitude of emotions; since we do not know what lies in the dark, who can say if it is bad? If we go into a cave, there could be carnivorous beasts hiding within, but there could also be just the tools we need to lead us to victory.

There is no simple definition for the shadow. There are nuances here that can be difficult to explain and even comprehend. But it is important, particularly for the SSP, to understand the shadow in this manner. It is not something to be feared, but something to be accepted and mined for the "diamonds" it carries; our deep truths lying within. I would like to reiterate this in the context of the Savior/Shadow Principle; I do not mean to insinuate this is a general meaning, though I have seen similar observations from various disciplines, e.g., Tarot, Psychology, Mythology, etc.

The light represents the conscious part of us. The "hero" archetype can fall under this; it is the masculine, outwardly focused energy within us all. We can have ideas burst forth from our subconscious—that is, the shadow or the dark. They are then "birthed" into the conscious mind—that is the light. Finally, those ideas can be practically integrated into our lives. The SSP could serve as a catalyst and a facilitator to this process.

While we now have a nice introduction to the concept of duality, we will continue with that idea and discuss archetypes. The concept of archetypes was another informative discovery for me while on my spiritual journey. We will also discuss the relationship of duality and archetypes, which is deeper than may be recognized at first glance.

Chapter V:

Archetypes

From my study of various pantheons during my time as a ChristoPagan, I began to see resemblance among the deities of different cultures. For instance, I saw similarities between Jesus, Chiron, and Buddha.

We can access collective human knowledge by researching various religions and myths. We can learn the complexities of being human from the deities of old and their accompanying stories. Through this type of study, we can understand more about ourselves, human nature, and how we can grow to become the *hero* of our own life *stories*.

A famous concept that shows this process is Joseph Campbell's "Hero's Journey," also referred to as the "monomyth"—a synthesis of common themes throughout worldwide mythologies and religions. If you are a fan of Tarot, you will see some similarities with the "Fool's Journey" of the Major Arcana. The Hero's Journey follows the hero from the beginning of a voyage, through the trials and tribulations he encounters, until his ultimate success. As Campbell states, "The standard path of the mythological adventure of the hero is a magnification of the formula represented in the rites of passage: *separation–initiation–return:* which might be named the nuclear unit of the monomyth" (23). Each of those three sections can be broken down into subsets; not all those subsets are present in every myth, but this overall formula is present (Campbell 28-29). One could study the Hero's Journey for insight on how to improve their life. Also, the Hero's Journey has been an asset to many writers over time; George Lucas has famously spoken of how it helped him write Star Wars.

When you discuss archetypes, you must bring up the works of Carl G. Jung, Founder of Analytical Psychology. One way Jung described archetypes was as "essentially an unconscious content that is altered by becoming conscious and by being perceived, and it takes its colour from the individual consciousness in which it happens to appear" (Jung, *The Archetypes* 5).

We can look at the archetype of the "Mother"—a collective archetype we are each familiar with and have our own unique perspectives on. There are additional archetypes he has discussed throughout his writings, for example, the Child, the Hero, and the Trickster. Each of these has a deep instinctual place in human understanding, per the collective unconscious we all share according to his theories—and individually, we have ideas of what they mean and represent. Jung has written a significant amount related to archetypes, mythologies, religions, and spirituality, the application of these in a clinical-type setting, etc. I highly recommend further research into his works if those topics interest you.

Archetypes are essentially examples of positive or negative energies that we can emulate or avoid to better our lives. In the following section, we will discuss a set of archetypes that will show how they can be interpreted, and how they can be seen as models of behavior. These are ones we all understand: Parents.

Parental Archetypes: Limiting or Expanding

Harkening back to the earlier discussion on duality, it is interesting that these archetypes also possess it. I feel good representations of this can be seen in the Mother and Father archetypes (we will continue with the traditional view of these energies as described earlier. Of course, these are not limited to biological sex, as we all have feminine and masculine energies within). These are simplified examples. Each parental archetype can be seen as having an "expanding" or "limiting" parental style (also representing light or shadow, respectively) in relation to their children: A mother or father can have an expanding effect—this is the parent who supports their child in becoming a functioning adult; this parent sees their child as an individual. Then there is the mother or father who possesses limiting energies—this is the parent who does not see their child as an individual and inhibits their growth in becoming a healthy and thriving adult.

To illustrate further, the expanding maternal figure represents a nurturing, feelings-based energy. This is the mother who believes in her child, gives unconditional love, and is emotionally supportive. Such behaviors allow for emotional stability, the ability to trust others, and additional positive results for the child. Of course, this is an archetype we are all familiar with; it is the positive mother role we have experienced, seen on television or in movies, etc.

The limiting maternal figure represents destructive energy, the opposite of the expanding energy. This is exemplified by viewing their child as a possession, being abusive, only providing love and attention when certain conditions are met, etc. This creates insecurity and can have a limiting effect on the child's development.

Like the expanding maternal figure, the expanding fatherly figure facilitates the growth of the child as an individual, but in a more outwardly focused way. Through his strength and hard work, the father provides a safe environment for the family so the child can develop. He encourages the child to be accountable for their actions, to make their own mark on the world, to grow into a responsible adult, etc. The acknowledgment page of this very book holds an example of this energy. For your convenience, I have included my acknowledgment message below:

> This book is dedicated to my father, David. With his support and encouragement, I was able to find the courage to write this book. Thanks Dad!

For some time, I was on the fence about writing this book. I was concerned about how others would view the material I presented and how they would view me as well. I know some of the comparisons I have made in these pages and the overall subject matter could be deemed very controversial, at best. However, my dad was very kind and encouraged me to share my ideas so others could learn from my experiences and perspective. After much thought, I agreed with his viewpoint and began writing this book.

From my own example, you can see the expanding energy at play by my father emboldening me to take a chance. This energy is about heartening the child to be brave, go out into the world, and become an adult in one's own right. I was able to write this book and fully realize a dream I had. From this experience, I have been able to grow into myself more. That is thanks to my father for cheering me on (Thanks again, Dad! ☺).

I would also like to add that my father did NOT know about the material I was presenting in this book. I gave him a very broad explanation, but he really did not know the specifics. This is another continuation of the expanding theme; my father was inspiring me to go out on my own to develop my voice. He ultimately motivated me not to be a carbon copy of him, not to be who he or other people want me to be, but to be who I truly am.

Now, using the limiting fatherly archetype as an example, that would be an overbearing energy. Think of a father who would want to know all about my book, read through and approve of what I would say, and maybe tell me not to write it but to do something in line with his vision. This could result in writing a new book on a topic that the limiting father figure would pick! The energy displayed here is a neutering or lessening energy; it does not allow the child to mature. It is like the shadow, dark, or limiting version of the mother archetype we just discussed. Again, the result limits the child's growth.

Fortunately, I encountered the expanding energies with my father and was able to achieve greater self-actualization. But you can see how both energies of the Father archetype could play out and their repercussions. One energy positively pushes the individual to expand, while the other negatively limits.

Another (and I believe perfect) example of the limiting fatherly energy can be seen in the Greek myth of Daphne and Apollo. The story begins with Apollo—or Phoebus, upsetting Cupid, who then shoots Apollo with a dart, causing him to fall in love. He also shoots Daphne, a beautiful water nymph, with an arrow, causing her to be disinterested in love. Daphne was also the daughter of the river god Peneus, who had been encouraging her to marry and have children. Apollo romantically pursued the young woman, and because of her lack of interest, she fled from him. In fleeing, she became more beautiful to Apollo, strengthening his adoration. Daphne called out to her father to save her, and upon hearing her cries, transformed the young woman into a laurel tree, which by the way, became Apollo's favorite (Ovid, "Daphne and Phoebus—lines 452-524"; "Daphne and Phoebus—lines 525-566").

Now, if we look at this myth in a personal development way, we can see this as an example of limiting fatherly energy (Campbell 52). For the sake of this exercise, we will set aside Cupid's arrows. As we grow older, it is natural to date, marry, and create a family of our own. I know what you are thinking, not everyone wants to marry! That is true, of course. However, it is important to at least gain some exposure to romantic relationships, i.e., dating, to make educated decisions. The decision to marry is a life-long one and should be treated with the utmost respect. Also, people change; what once was an absolute for someone can change as they age. I know that has happened to me plenty of times!

Peneus turning Daphne into a laurel tree has, in effect, *frozen* her; she is now stuck in perpetual young womanhood, unable to progress to the next level (Campbell 52). It isn't just that she will not have a relationship with the god Apollo; she will not have a relationship with *anyone*. She will not grow past this state; the once beautiful young woman will now stay a laurel tree.

Due to Daphne's fear of romantic pursuit, she decides to be kept safe by her father, to be locked into the *daughter* role, and to have him save her. By answering her cries, he limits her. It may feel to him as if he is doing the right thing, that he is *saving* his daughter, but he is actually stunting her growth. A proper response would be to encourage her to be open to suitors, not necessarily to the god Apollo, of course, but that she be open to this natural progression in life. This progression is a common marker in the lives of young adults everywhere. This story shows the young woman, frozen in her child-like innocence due to a limiting father, as the *forever daughter* (Campbell 52).

There are some macro-level similarities to the popularly mentioned "Peter Pan" energies we attribute to adult males. While there are definite differences, they exhibit similar "never growing up" energies. Both have given up on progressing to the next level of adulthood and are still living out youthful roles.

These two examples show the result of a limiting or expanding parent upon a child. Of course, there are a multitude of examples from mythology that can be presented, including those with a male child and the mother. However, these are sufficient to show the effects of both energies, regardless of the biological sex of the parent or child. The actions of the parent will greatly impact the child, ultimately resulting in their maturity—from an expanding parenting style—or immaturity— from a limiting parenting style. I would also like to add that even though families were discussed, these energies can be present in any relationship, whether related or not.

In the following chapter, we will discuss Hekate, a goddess with a rich history. I will give introductory information for a foundational understanding of her nature. Per the information presented in this chapter, in addition to her mythology, she can exhibit some of the positive and negative motherly energies we have discussed. I will also briefly explain my interpretation of them per the Savior/Shadow Principle.

Chapter VI:

An Overview of Hekate:

A Complex Goddess

Hekate is a unique goddess in that she has been a part of many cultures throughout time. Because she is an ancient goddess, there are different stories of her lineage. However, she is commonly referred to as the daughter of

Asteria and Perses. Hekate is also a Titan—which are deities that predate the Olympians. As we've discussed earlier, she is a very popular goddess among modern-day Pagans. She also was a figure in "the Renaissance...the Byzantine and Roman Empires, Hellenistic, Classical and Archaic Greece through into the Greek Dark Ages – and beyond." There is record of her "for at least three thousand years" (d'Este 19).

As a by-product of her enduring history, she has been syncretized with numerous goddesses. Through this, she has gained different attributes by introducing new areas of worship. Below is a list of other names she has been known by:

Chthonia *('earthly one')*

Dadouchos *('torch-bearer')*

Enodia *('of the ways')*

Kleidouchos *('key-bearer')*,

Kourotrophos *('child's nurse')*

Phosphorous *('light-bearer')*.

Propolos *('companion')*

Propylaia *('before the gate')*,

Soteira *('saviour')*

Triformis *('three-bodied')*

Trioditis *('of the three ways')*

(d'Este 19-20).

There are quite a few names here! Throughout history, Hekate was frequently associated with crossroads and other liminal places (which have been historically associated with witches and magic), being a mediator between the physical and spiritual worlds (more on this momentarily), childbirth, key-bearer, etc.; she is a deity of change.

As for my personal thoughts on Hekate, I mentioned earlier that I viewed her as a goddess of *truth*. She has a varied history, which lends to this: she was a goddess of darker aspects of life—e.g., witchcraft and magic (like curses, for example, which suggest the limiting energies as mentioned earlier). The truth of their existence; her role as truth-teller in the Persephone myth (also a nurturer, like the expanding motherly energies discussed in the previous chapter; more on this soon), just to name a few. I also found the *truth* of her similarities to elements of Christianity quite interesting.

Macro-Level Similarities

An interesting idea to note is that Hekate bears a macro-level similarity to the triune God of Christianity. For example, there is the triple nature of Hekate; she was even represented as having three heads. This bears some similarity to the triune nature of God through the Father, Son, and Holy Spirit. Also, God the Father went through changes throughout the Bible; he was a vengeful, angry God in the Old Testament and more father-like and forgiving in the New Testament. Hekate also underwent a similar transformation in the Chaldean Oracles, as she was a goddess to witches, then became a more benevolent figure (Johnston 1)[1].

While in current popular culture, she is associated more as a dark goddess, the view I am focused on looks at Hekate as a universal goddess. The Chaldean Oracles we just discussed substantiate this view; the Oracles were a collection of spiritual writings popular in antiquity. For instance, her "importance in the Chaldean system is not based exclusively on her role as a goddess of the Underworld" but also "mediating between and dividing two portions of the universe...the "Sensible" and "Intelligible" worlds" or rather the world of

---

humans and that of the divine (Johnston 11; Dillon 394)[2]. In this system, "Hekate was identified with the Platonic Cosmic Soul" (Johnston 1)[3]. The Chaldean Oracles characterized her as a "Savior" goddess, one that is a connection to the heavens and the earth—the bridge between. This is also a macro-level similarity to Jesus, who also acts as a bridge. This concept evokes the famous scripture, John 14:6 (NKJV): "Jesus said to him, "I am the way, the truth, and the life. No one comes to the Father except through Me.""

---

[2] Hekate Soteira by Sarah Iles Johnston. © 1990 The American Philological Association. Reproduced with permission of the Licenser through PLSclear.

[3] Hekate Soteira by Sarah Iles Johnston. © 1990 The American Philological Association. Reproduced with permission of the Licenser through PLSclear.

Hekate is also frequently associated with fire. She is commonly depicted with torches, as she had in the Persephone myth. Fire is also widely referenced throughout the Bible. One can recall God descending on Mount Sinai as fire in Exodus 19:18, the burning bush in Exodus 3:1-4:17, believers to be baptized "with the Holy Spirit and fire" by Jesus in Matthew 3:11 (NKJV), and the list goes on. There is another similarity to Jesus, the Son of God Most High—as Hekate was viewed as "born of the Father, the Supreme God of the Chaldean system" (Johnston 50)[4]. Both are associated with angels, with Hekate and angels being discussed in "the

---

[4] Hekate Soteira by Sarah Iles Johnston. © 1990 The American Philological Association. Reproduced with permission of the Licenser through PLSclear.

Greek Magical Papyri and the Chaldean Oracles" (d'Este 107-108). Divine names commonly used to depict God in Judaism, Solomon, and potentially Jesus and God the Father (Christianity), have been found alongside Hekate in various spells (from the aforementioned Greek Magical Papyri and other sources) and talismans from antiquity (d'Este 163-168). Finally, we have all heard the story of the birth of Jesus and the gifts from the three wise men; two of the three gifts were frankincense and myrrh. In summoning Hekate for rituals, a concoction was made that also included frankincense and myrrh (Johnston

88)[5]. Granted, these two items are well-known to have been popular in antiquity, but it is still quite interesting that both were related to each of these deities.

Another similarity from the Chaldean Oracles: "The fact that many of the Oracles were spoken in the first person by a god or goddess...supported the illusion of divine authorship" (Johnston 4)[6]. This is quite interesting and similar to Christianity. While I was attending a Christian University (I possess an M.A. in Biblical Studies), I learned that the books of the Bible were attributed to

---

[5] Hekate Soteira by Sarah Iles Johnston. © 1990 The American Philological Association. Reproduced with permission of the Licenser through PLSclear.

[6] Hekate Soteira by Sarah Iles Johnston. © 1990 The American Philological Association. Reproduced with permission of the Licenser through PLSclear.

"authors"—i.e., Book of Mark, Book of John, etc.—to give them prestige and perceived validity because of their names, not because said person necessarily authored them; attributing works to others was common practice for writings in these earlier periods. Though this is not pertinent information for the SSP, it is interesting to note.

Just to reiterate, these are "macro" level similarities. In no way am I saying they are equivalent deities, or anything similar. These are very high-level similarities— synchronicities—that inspired me to dig deeper; they helped me create the theoretical foundation for which the application function of the Savior/Shadow Principle can occur. Also, this is not exhaustive. This is meant only as an introduction to the concepts.

Now that we've had a broad introduction to Hekate, we will discuss the myth of the abduction of Persephone. Hekate plays an important role in this myth. I also believe this myth shows her "savior goddess" energy.

The Abduction of Persephone Myth

This story, part of the Homeric Hymns, is paramount to later chapters. Here, I will summarize the myth, though I encourage you to read the full version at your leisure. You will find the citation information under the "Works Cited" section.

The goddess Demeter (Goddess of Harvest) and her daughter Persephone (Goddess of Spring and the Underworld—both designations coming from this story) were enjoying the outdoors with several of the daughters of Oceanus; they were playing and picking flowers. As they were enjoying themselves, Hades burst from an opening in the ground to grab the young lady and steal her to the Underworld.

Persephone cried out to be saved, but the only ones who heard her were the goddess Hekate, referred to as *tender-hearted*, and Lord Helios. Demeter could not find her daughter, and Hekate came and told her that she had heard Persephone's cries but did not see who had kidnapped the young woman.

They then went to Helios, who told them that Hades had taken her with permission from Persephone's father, Zeus!

This greatly upset Demeter, and she avoided the other gods and goddesses. She hid, causing a blight on the harvests, which was devastating to mankind (for those interested in comparative mythology, there is a similarity here to the story of the Japanese sun goddess, Amaterasu; see the end of the "Works Cited" section for additional information). Zeus sent messengers but to no avail. He then sent Hermes to retrieve Persephone from Hades as the famine worsened. He was able to get her, but through trickery, Hades made Persephone eat a single pomegranate seed. While she was returned to Demeter, who was thrilled to have her daughter back and restored the harvests, that small seed tied Persephone to the Underworld. While she could spend two-thirds of the year with her mother, she had to spend a third of the year down with Hades. Hekate becomes a "minister and companion" to Persephone from that point onward ("Hymn 2 to Demeter").

The Importance of the Persephone Myth

While this story explains the changing seasons, it also shows us the realities of growing up. Persephone could not remain a girl forever, staying solely by her mother's side. Just like all of us, she had to become an adult with increased responsibilities. It was her destiny to become Queen of the Underworld alongside Hades. While life transitions are difficult, we each must leave the old (childhood in this case), to go out into the world and become who we are meant to be.

As for Hekate, we can see a kind and helpful side to her. She is referred to as "tender-hearted" and is there to assist Demeter in finding out where her daughter is. She also assists Persephone with descending into and ascending from the Underworld each year. As discussed earlier, Hekate is associated with torches; the full version of the above myth even mentions them. She lights the way into the depths and out, back into the light. Hekate is there for Persephone as a helper, protector, and friend. She is a positive motherly-type figure while Persephone is away from her actual mother.

This is also a good representation of Hekate as a symbol of truth. She comes to

Demeter to tell her what she knows about her daughter's abduction. Hekate delivers the uncomfortable truth, torch in hand, to Demeter; the torch bringing light or awareness.

Since we have been introduced to Hekate and her nature from the Persephone myth, it is now time to move on and discuss Jesus as well. I will share with you some information on him that facilitates understanding the SSP. The following chapter will present unique information on a deity that we all at least have some familiarity with.

Chapter VII:

An Overview of Jesus:

A Non-Traditional Take

The topic of Jesus is so vast that it is difficult to narrow down the information for a single chapter. Different denominations have unique thoughts and interpretations, and countless books, articles, studies, etc., have been written on every possible aspect of his life and ministry. There is just so much material, interesting and worthwhile it may be, that is just outside the scope of this text.

However, I encourage you to read them if you are interested. The differences in opinion are fascinating; you will find that many mainstream thoughts are consensus, not pure fact (this is true of history in general). Also, Christianity is not a monolith, and there is quite a diversity of thought among the various denominations. Reading these materials can dramatically change one's worldview on history, religion, and academic study in general.

In this chapter, I have decided to share my personal experiences and information I studied while practicing ChristoPaganism. Both will give a different, nontraditional view of Jesus. I remember some people I encountered had difficulty understanding such a path. Of course, depending on their experiences with Christianity, this is understandable; some denominations are more "hard-line" than others. By sharing this information, I hope to shed light on these alternative views.

This information also shows that since this path has a lot of personal freedom, one will encounter a lot of different viewpoints; you can find two self-described ChristoPagans who don't agree on very much! But I will share the ideas I found were fairly common...not just from ChristoPagans, but contemporary Pagans as well.

At the end of this chapter, I will also share some general information regarding the post-crucifixion of Jesus, particularly of "Sheol." This is a primary focus of the Christianized SSP, so some discussion is warranted here. Like the introduction to Hekate, this will be a general overview.

First, I'd like to harken back to the discussion on my ChristoPagan path and the idea of *Source*. As I mentioned previously, my practice could be defined as soft polytheism; I believed all gods and goddesses were one, and the deities we see in the various world religions were manifestations of different energies from the divine Source. I met other ChristoPagans, in addition to Pagans, who also thought this way. Of course, this makes it easy for one to worship deities from different pantheons. I have met other ChristoPagans and Pagans who believed in hard polytheism. This means they believe that each god and goddess is a unique divine entity, which is just to remind you of the diversity of thought in these groups. However, many of my beliefs were not unique to me, and I encountered plenty of others who held similar ones.

Earlier, I mentioned a book titled *ChristoPaganism: An Inclusive Path* by Joyce and River Higginbotham. An interesting part of this book is that it contains interviews with fifteen people who fall under the "ChristoPagan" umbrella; they may not refer to themselves by that term, but they were each practicing a path that could be described by it. They came from different backgrounds, and while none of their beliefs were exactly the same, there were macro-level similarities in their spiritual practices. I would describe each of them as "religious seekers" like myself; they were interested in other religions and spiritual practices as a whole. In fact, their stories bear some similarities to mine! I would say these people all had an openness towards new religions and experiences. Some practiced Christianity in parallel with other spiritual practices, some practiced a blended path (I did this as well), and some were believers in a divine creative power similar to *Source* that I discussed earlier. However, these individuals followed the pull towards learning about Pagan-related teachings and possessed a connection to Jesus and Christianity; they each followed a path they felt was uniquely for them. I would say the fellow ChristoPagans I encountered while practicing bore similarities to the individuals in this book (183-274).

Another very insightful book is *Jesus through Pagan Eyes: Bridging Neopagan Perspectives with a Progressive Vision of Christ* by Reverend Mark Townsend. If non-traditional Christian and contemporary Pagan viewpoints interest you, I highly recommend this book. It has a lot of interesting information. Reverend Townsend's personal story and scholarly information will be useful to those interested in ChristoPaganism or just a non-traditional view of Christianity.

In this book, Reverend Townsend introduces an interesting concept relating to

Jesus. It was that he can be viewed in three different ways, or "personas:"

> 1. The *human* Jesus of Nazareth
> 2. The *divinised* Jesus Christ of the Church (whom scholars often refer to as the Christ of Faith)
> 3. The *universal* Mythic or Cosmic Christ (Townsend 14).

The first two are self-explanatory. But the third? When I read this for the first time, it was a new concept for me as well. The third persona "refers to the universal spark of deity manifested within all people and all things" and "is not the possession of the Church" (15).

Of the Pagans interviewed by Reverend Townsend, many had a similar divided view of Jesus as well. Some even worked with Jesus in their spiritual practice, too! However, similar to the ChristoPagans interviewed in the earlier book, many seemed to have a more macro-level view of religion. They mentioned the commonalities between Jesus and other deities in his Christ-like role. Again, a very educational read for those interested (225-325).

Lastly, a book by Adelina St. Clair called *The Path of a Christian Witch* also shares her blended path and thoughts of Jesus. Her path is similar to what I had practiced, a meld of Christianity and Wicca. In the book, she states: "Simply put, Christians are those who follow the teachings of Christ" (St. Clair 47). I feel that she nicely summarizes her views on who can be a Christian; she is concerned with Jesus' teachings and not dogma from various denominations, politics, etc. (47). She also discusses similarities between Christianity and the Wiccan path in this text as well. It is a very interesting read for those intrigued by such a practice.

Ultimately, you can see that some unique beliefs exist among these groups. I believe this is the fundamental issue that acts as a roadblock to understanding. A lack of exposure to these different ideas when discussing Jesus in relation to the SSP and ChristoPaganism. I hope this brief introduction is impactful in counteracting that.

The Concept of Sheol

Finally, I'd like to share a bit about Sheol; it is imperative to the wholly Christianized version of the SSP. While it can mean different things, we're focusing on the idea of Sheol as a place. Here is an excerpt from an earlier paper I wrote about the SSP that I feel sums up this concept perfectly:

> Sheol was the place one's soul went to after death, whether righteous or unrighteous. The formal Heaven and Hell we know of as modern-day Christians was created after Jesus went to Sheol – after his death on the cross – and released those whom were righteous in Sheol to take their

rightful place in Heaven, while the unrighteous were left in what we now refer to as Hell (McAfee, "The Savior/Shadow Principle").

We have covered a lot in these last few chapters! Not only have we been introduced to ChristoPaganism, but to the ancient goddess Hekate and a non-traditional view of Jesus. Since we now understand these topics, we can start discussing the SSP itself.

Chapter VIII:

The Savior/Shadow Principle

We've spoken so much about deities, duality, and spirituality. What does it all mean? It was to lay the groundwork for this discussion here. There are different steps to this; there is the theoretical portion, where we must know the deities, their history, etc.; then there is the application portion, which I would describe as a guided meditation.

From the theoretical, we have a sense of who Hekate and Jesus are and how they can have a unique interplay based on their similarities. We understand duality and how that can be applied across many different subjects. We understand the concept of archetypes and how they can be useful models of behavior in life.

How does this manifest into practical application? First, we want to get into a comfortable, meditative state. You could lie down, sit, or do whatever works best for you. Make sure you are in a quiet area where you will be undisturbed; light candles or incense if you'd like as well. From there, you can recollect the story of Persephone and Hekate's savior and friend roles in that myth. Think of the kindness and the helping energy of her actions toward Persephone and her mother, Demeter. Allow yourself to take Persephone's place; instead of going into the Underworld per the myth, you are going into the deep cave within.

Now, imagine yourself accepting the kindness being offered by Hekate. Imagine her being your protector, holding torches to light your way, assisting you on this inward journey. There is no judgment here; it is safe. You have a powerful goddess by your side! Allow yourself to bathe in these positive feelings.

Once you really feel the kindness, protection, and safety from Hekate, you can think of anything, like the situations troubling you. There is no need to feel any defensiveness, no need to hide from any uncomfortable truths. Imagine that you and Hekate are walking in a deep cavern within you, full of diamonds waiting to be mined—these being truths about yourself, creative ideas, etc. Think of them as the information you seek being held within you.

After you have spent sufficient time thinking and evaluating the information that presents itself, imagine yourself walking with Hekate toward a light that is guiding you outside of a tunnel. Now, you can imagine Jesus pulling you from the cavern and onto the ground; you have the diamonds within that you have mined. You also feel safe and loving kindness from this interaction. But now, with these *jewels* you have discovered, you and Jesus ascend to the heavens. You can liken this to bringing what you have learned about yourself and taking that information— those *diamonds*— into your conscious awareness for practical application. This is essentially a process similar to Jung's idea of "individuation"—the process of becoming the unique individual you are. I like viewing the "ascension" as rising to a new and improved version of oneself.

Now, this isn't a *one-and-done* process. You may have to do this meditation many times before you can fully tap into those positive feelings to look within; it may take you several times before you can form that information into a cohesive plan for self-betterment. However, with time and practice, I believe this technique could be helpful to you.

I also don't want to suggest that once you're able to accomplish success with this, you're done; you've grown, and that's it! I have done this technique many times and continue to use it (though it has gotten easier for me to access the positive feelings, so I may not need the imaginative portion every time). I don't have everything figured out, and I continue to work on myself. There is always capacity for growth, no matter our age or level of maturity. In addition, just because we achieve something once doesn't mean it's forever done; we can regress and need to revisit areas of our lives that we once felt confident in.

This process can allow us to delve into the shadow, which is complex and can rustle up negative feelings. From Jung himself,

The shadow is a moral problem that challenges the whole ego-personality, for no one can become conscious of the shadow without considerable moral effort. To become more conscious of it involves recognizing the dark aspects as present and real. This act is the essential condition for any kind of self-knowledge, and it therefore, as a rule, meets with considerable resistance (Jung, *Aion* 8).

The SSP technique is meant to counteract this resistance; that is why the loving, kind, and protective energies of these two deities must be focused upon. I agree with Jung's assessment of shadow side traits:

He also felt the traits that reside in our Shadow side are more emotional, and cause the individual to behave "more or less, like a primitive" who unfortunately, is a "passive victim of his affects but also singularly incapable of moral judgment" (Jung, *Aion* 8-9). However, with some honest effort, at least parts of the Shadow side can be assimilated into the conscious/ego to some degree, to ultimately become a better, more integrated human being (McAfee, "The Savior/Shadow Principle").

Some of the shadow traits can be resolved. This will be discussed in further detail later, but to harken back to Sheol as an example, after Jesus was crucified, that is where his spirit went. It is like the Jewish Underworld, where he then freed the righteous while leaving the unrighteous. Again, it was this action that created the Heaven and Hell of Christianity. We can liken Sheol to the shadow; we can resolve or free some behaviors, while we need to leave others in order to manage. By working with these behaviors, we can become more whole.

I don't know about you, but I like to hear stories about how a technique can be applied to understand how it works. Below is one I created to illustrate how the SSP could be used. Also, I will share with you how this technique allowed me to tap into positive changes and better my life.

An Example of SSP Application

Let's imagine an individual currently experiencing some difficulties in life; we can refer to this person as Sam. Sam works at a cake decorating factory. For the sake of the example, let's assume the cakes are baked and frosted at a different facility, then sent to where Sam works to be decorated, packaged, and shipped to stores. Sam's job is to pipe a yellow circle in the middle of the cakes, and then it goes on to another person. We'll call this person Alice, who pipes the flower petals. The completed cake then goes to someone who packages it: Ralph, and is then loaded on a truck by Jen to be delivered to grocery stores for sale.

Sam begins to lose focus on the tasks at hand. Instead of piping the circle for the flower correctly on the cake, he begins haphazardly putting it off-center. Sam is feeling stressed. He has been having problems with his loved ones: his parents, friends, and girlfriend. He has focused on these problems, so much so that his work is suffering because of it. When Sam does not do his job accurately, Alice cannot complete her task of adding the flower petals and must send the cake back to Sam to be fixed.

A few sent back here and there are not a problem. However, Alice continuously must send the cakes back. Ralph notices that the number of cakes he is packaging has dwindled, and when he does get them, he is swamped and must wrap them expeditiously. Jen has noticed this as well, as the number of completed cakes is not the same as usual, affecting her deliveries. It is getting so bad that there is a bottleneck, and shipments are not being made to the grocery stores as they are accustomed to.

Because of this, they have complained to factory management and have threatened to cancel orders. Management has discussed this with the factory, and it is known among the workers that the issue is Sam. Sam is embarrassed and upset; he is disappointed with himself and his performance. Sam's coworkers, Alice, Ralph, and Jen, are upset with him, as his negligence could prove detrimental to the whole company. This would affect not only Sam, of course, but also them, as management may lay off employees. Ultimately, their families would pay the price. Alice, Ralph, and Jen have all but ostracized Sam.

Sam is trying his best to keep up, but his negative self-image and stress continue to grow. His coworkers' obvious resentment is just compounding his problems. All the negativity has only worsened his home life, as he is arguing with his loved ones even more. To alleviate the pressure, he has turned to drinking and partying.

Sam's now staying out late, spending a lot of money at bars, and going to work hungover. His performance has continued to deteriorate, in addition to his relationships in and out of work.

His self-esteem has hit rock-bottom, and there is no end to his suffering in sight.

During this time, he is introduced to the Savior/Shadow Principle. He can imagine Hekate walking with him through the darkness to his inner Underworld, where his negative traits, all the things he is running away from, reside. He can be honest with himself, feeling safe with the goddess by his side, torches in hand to illuminate the truth. He knows he has had a lot of interpersonal problems lately and that his nightly activities are not helping matters any.

What would improve his current situation? Well, first, stop partying and drinking immediately. To be honest, the fleeting relief he gains from it pales in comparison to the guilt and physical malaise he feels afterward. If that were eradicated from his life, what else would need revamping? Work could definitely be better for him. What would improve that area of his life? If he elevated his work performance, his coworkers would react more positively toward him. He misses the time he had pleasant work relationships with Alice, Ralph, and Jen.

How did I get into this mess to begin with? Why did my work quality suffer? He asks himself. It began to lessen as he became increasingly stressed with his personal relationships. This realization makes him ponder them in greater detail. Sam identifies that his family, friends, and girlfriend were upsetting him. What is the reason for that? Are there multiple reasons?

After some additional thinking, he recognizes the stress from his family was due to his parents' financial difficulties. Sam is happy to help, but the amount and frequency of their requests for money have become excessive. He has been supporting them for a while, and it is causing problems with his girlfriend. He tries to go out with friends to alleviate his stress, but she resents this and wants him to stay home. Sam's friends do not like her as they feel she constantly causes drama and regularly berate him to end the relationship.

Sam recognizes this is a multi-layered problem and cannot be fixed easily. Even though it is difficult, he reviews his relationships and resolves to be honest with himself regarding how he would like each to be. First, Sam would like to stop sending money to his parents; it makes him feel guilty to think that, but if he is honest with himself, the money he gives them creates difficulties. He would also like his girlfriend to be more supportive, and while she has reason to be upset about financial issues, she could be more understanding of this difficult situation. Also, he does not want to stay at home with her all the time and feels it is healthy if they both go out with their friends sometimes.

As for his friends, he is happy to hang out with them but would prefer if they could stop harping on him to break up with his girlfriend. It weighs on him a lot, and there are more issues they are unfamiliar with. He understands it is fine for them to have opinions and welcomes their advice, but there must be an endpoint. Sam feels that his problems with his girlfriend are always hanging over him because his friends constantly talk about them. He hangs out with them to have fun, to escape from his problems, not to continually discuss them.

Sam now recognizes the issues he has been having and feels lighter from defining his problems. He also feels better by simply acknowledging what he wants. Sam could accept his current situation more by visiting his inner Underworld and accepting non-judgmental self-kindness, as exemplified by the story of Persephone, likening himself to her traveling into the dark with Hekate lighting the way. Instead of getting upset with himself for performing poorly at work, he accepted reality and was honest with himself about how he could fix it. He was honest with himself about the current status of his relationships and how they could be improved. He stopped repressing his feelings; he accepted them fully and did not allow them to take over his mind. Thus, he can now rationally consider what he wants and how to rectify reality and the ideal in his mind.

Now, Sam has a mental blueprint of how to get out of the predicament he's in. He imagines himself being pulled out of the darkness by Jesus himself, shining brightly and bringing him into the Heavens; Sam envisions himself ascending to the light, becoming an improved version of himself. While it will be a lot of work, the self-honesty he achieved has given him the strength to pursue a better life. Sam first talks with his parents and lets them know of his difficulties with giving them money. His parents were unaware of the stress it was putting on him and formulate alternative plans to remedy their financial issues.

Sam and his girlfriend then discuss their issues. While many raw feelings are involved, they each have a better appreciation of the other's mindset. While nothing gets resolved immediately, they decide to move forward and communicate issues without shouting and arguing. Whatever the future holds for them, they now share greater awareness and opportunity to strengthen their bond.

Sam also talks with his friends and lets them know he will be going out at set times, i.e., on the weekends, and that he is currently working on things with his girlfriend. He draws a boundary and wants them to respect his relationship. His friends understand his perspective, and they agree.

Sam feels an incredible weight off himself and has a better attitude. Since he does not drink and stay out late every night, he can improve the quality of his work. His coworkers and, more importantly, the grocery stores notice that they receive cakes as usual and are no longer complaining. Things are running much smoother for the factory, and Sam's coworkers have begun warming up to him again. His life has improved tremendously.

This example, while over-simplified, better illuminates the processes I have tried to introduce via the SSP. One person, i.e., Sam, was the source of the problems affecting the factory. Is it possible for a company's issues to be due to one person? Sure, but it's not probable. Company culture, complicit coworkers, etc., are likely influencers among a list of other potential variables. While this example is not the most realistic (Sam also was able to tap into his truths very quickly), it reveals the interplay of personal and professional issues and how self-honesty can help improve a multitude of problems. It also illustrates how the SSP can be practically applied to help bring about that self-honesty and reflection needed for positive changes.

Will all the relationships work out positively? No one can know for sure. While the example seems very optimistic, it leaves everything open-ended. Sam's parents could decide not to follow through with their alternative plans, he and his girlfriend could break up, and his friends could disregard the boundaries he had set with them. Sam himself could regress at work and be fired. But it does illustrate that talking with everyone allows for greater understanding and gives them the *chance* of an improved relationship. This example shows that by being honest with yourself, you can be honest with others.

An Example from My Own Life

I am sharing this technique—a system to spark self-compassion and self-honesty—because it ultimately worked for me. During the time I came up with this, I was full of self-doubt and unsure of the roads I wanted to take. I was upset at disappointing situations and, frankly, myself, too. With all these chaotic feelings swirling around inside of me, I felt utterly lost.

As I've said, this preceded, and even facilitated, the ChristoPagan period of my spiritual journey. As my spiritual path became a bit more established, I was able to really delve into the various deities and what they each symbolized to me. The stories of Hekate and Jesus inspired me and allowed me access to something I desperately needed: self-compassion. I needed the pressure I was putting on myself, the hurt from upsetting situations, the noise from the outer world, everything, to stop weighing on me. How can a person think of making their life more positive when they're weighed down with so much gunk?!

By meditating on the "compassionate" portion of these stories and allowing myself to imagine being the benefactor of their kindness, I could let go of the weight for a bit. As I continued these meditations, I was able to let go of more and more. I felt such comfort at those moments! After some time, I was able to start thinking of changes to improve my life.

The compassionate state I was able to bring about within allowed me to tap into deep self-honesty. It was a state in which I didn't judge myself, didn't allow critical inner voices to intervene, and could just focus on the questions and thoughts at hand. These stories, these deities, were symbols of compassion and kindness for me and inspired those feelings to arise within *myself*.

I just let the ideas spring forth on their own. I didn't battle them. I looked at myself objectively but through a lens of kindness. I gave thought to what I truly wanted out of life, not what I thought would make me a respectable member of society. Frankly, depending on where you live, that definition can change dramatically! It can be very silly, these corners we push ourselves in.

For several years prior, I was convinced I wanted to become a corporate wunderkind—a CEO following in the footsteps of Mark Zuckerberg (he and I are close in age, and it seemed like many in my age group, if not a majority, wanted to emulate his success). But I began accepting this was not for me, and that there were other areas of my life I was overly focused on, including the outer world. I needed to listen to my own heart!

It wasn't just around career, but different areas of my life in general. I wanted to reignite an old hobby of mine and make art: draw, paint, etc. I loved art as a kid; I was often complimented on my art and even won a big contest in elementary school! I had a natural ability but hadn't picked up a drawing pencil in years. I wanted to correct that. I wanted to become a better artist. I wanted to relive the magic and happiness art gave me when I was younger.

It was the first time in a while that I was able to get in touch with the authentic parts of me, what made me "Kimberly." Growing into adulthood, we must encounter different ideas, different ways of living, etc., to find our place in this world. This exposure is very important and integral to becoming well-adjusted adults. But the "popular" and "accepted" in a particular time can be overwhelming and put too much weight on your decisions. In those moments of self-reflection, it occurred to me how silly it was to give so much influence to such trivial ideas. We are each a unique individual; there has never been anyone exactly like us, and there never will be. Why put a damper on our real selves?

I also realized I needed to move forward toward becoming a writer through the SSP technique. I was committed to that journey but wanted to find my correct "lane." I began trying different writing genres to ensure I pursued what I truly loved. There was a lot of bumbling! I have written various articles on a multitude of subjects, short screenplays, poems, song lyrics, short stories, books...you name it, I've tried it!

However, it was during the global pandemic that I found the bravery to post my poems on Instagram and interact with other writers. Again, through diving into self, I embraced honesty and recognized I was intimidated; I knew a poetry community was there (though I didn't know anything past its existence), and was frightened that I wouldn't be accepted, people wouldn't like my work, etc. In the fall of 2020, I finally mustered up the courage to create an account and, shortly afterward, started posting my poetry.

Through the years that followed, I can't fully put into words how thankful I am for that decision. Seemingly small, it has given me so many tremendous gifts: I have been published many times, I have published books, and I have finally finished this book—my magnum opus (at least up to this point!). A poem of mine was posted on the John Lennon Wall in Prague, Czech Republic by the Poetizer app for the #WeStandWithU event in support of the Ukrainian people (a link will be shared at the end of the "Works Cited" section), and most importantly, I've met so many beautiful people from all around the world that I am proud to call friends. For me, being on Instagram has been the gift that keeps giving! No matter what the future holds, all these experiences are now precious memories I will cherish for the rest of my days. They have enriched my life and have made me excited for the years to come.

It also helped me achieve a new level of self-acceptance. I felt like something was missing in my life, though I couldn't place it. I have always felt like an *odd man out.* Not just visually being different, I am AmerAsian, but also in temperament. Meeting my fellow poets, I realize I am very similar to them all: I am sensitive, sentimental, passionate, can see the beauty in all things ("magic in the mundane"), can be suddenly overcome by inspiration, etc. I feel that I have found my place, my tribe: I am a Poet.

I also want to mention this book again, as it means so much to me. Like I said earlier, I spent a long time wondering if I should write it. But my dad gave me a lot of encouragement and confidence to move forward; getting on Instagram and all the positives that followed further sustained me to see this project through.

Plainly, the SSP technique has helped me tremendously. I have so many tangible examples of how it inspired me to be more honest with myself, which, allowed me to make changes for the better. Of course, I'm not perfect. I have plenty to work on and always will, but the SSP *has* improved my life. Because of the positive it has brought me, I believe it could also be helpful to others.

I hope this story about myself inspires you to find ways you can improve your life, and I also hope the SSP is helpful to you in achieving that. Something I have referenced throughout this book is self-honesty, so you can find what works best for you. I know the SSP in its original form may be a bit much for others to incorporate, fortunately, this technique can be modified to feature only Hekate or Jesus. Particularly if you are Pagan or Christian, one of these versions could work better for you. In the following chapters, we will revisit the SSP.

Chapter IX:

The Savior/Shadow Principle Redux I:
Hekate, a Complex Goddess

In this chapter, we will begin to see the flexibility of the SSP. From the original version with Hekate and Jesus, we can now easily interchange the two deities to create a version with only one. We will be focusing on the Persephone and Hades myth discussed earlier.

As a reminder, Persephone is kidnapped by Hades and taken to the Underworld, as he desires her. Persephone's mother, Demeter, is distraught over her missing daughter and cries for help. Out of all the gods and goddesses of the Greek pantheon, only one comes to her aid: Hekate. Through deception on the part of Hades, Persephone must return to him several months out of the year (she becomes Queen of the Underworld as well). It is Hekate who agrees to guide her descent into and ascent out of the Underworld by the light of her torches and stay with her during her time below.

In the original Savior/Shadow Principle, we discussed the Persephone and Hades myth, but it was the descent portion that was of interest. In this revisited version, we will only focus on Hekate's part of the myth: the descent into, accompaniment, and the ascent out of the Underworld with Persephone.

Per the story above, we can see Hekate as a helper to Demeter and Persephone. This is an important feature to note, as it is useful for the SSP and the duality comparison mentioned earlier. The helping actions are similar to the Christ energy portrayed by Jesus; a suffering servant-type energy. This version of the Savior/Shadow Principle could be especially useful to those who are not Christian, who are interested in Greek mythology, and to women. There appears to be a great interest in female deities currently, and this could be beneficial to those who resonate with feminine energies. Now, we will move on to the Jesus-specific version of the SSP.

Chapter X:

The Savior/Shadow Principle
Redux II: Jesus, the Christian Son of God

While we have discussed nontraditional views
of Jesus in the preceding chapters, this Jesus-
only version of the Savior/Shadow Principle
could be used by those who are mainstream
Christians; this is in line with traditional

viewings of Jesus. If you want to connect with your inner voice and are a mainstream Christian, this could work well for you.

So, instead of looking to Hekate and Persephone going into the Underworld as a metaphorical example of going inward, we can look at the full post-crucifixion story of Jesus instead. As we have discussed earlier, after Jesus was crucified and placed in his burial chamber, his spirit was sent to Sheol, similar to the Underworld. Jesus freed the souls meant for Heaven; this created Heaven and Hell. After Jesus was resurrected, he ascended to his rightful place in Heaven, at the right hand of God.

You could imagine yourself as one of the souls in Sheol, awaiting your moment of salvation. Then envision meeting Jesus, knowing you would be taken to live forever in Heaven. Think of the happiness that you would feel! To finally reach your eternal, incredibly positive, home. It would be nothing short of amazing! Accept the forgiveness that Jesus represents and look at yourself fully with the unconditional love he offers. Then, picture yourself ascending, leaving behind what you no longer need, allowing yourself to accept light and growth—to become the person you are meant to be, i.e., your rightful place in Heaven.

I would also like to add that if you're interested in this version of the meditation, instead of seeing "left-behind" behaviors as in Hell, I would think of it as a "reset." These behaviors that need mitigation and management or that you hope to work on later are still in

Sheol; they are awaiting you in the future. I think this aids in relieving negative connotations, which can breed discomfort and avoidance behaviors, and still foster the self-compassion we hope to achieve.

Ultimately, it is the process of the Savior/Shadow Principle that needs to be focused on. Whichever version allows you to connect with the feelings of self-compassion and self-honesty is the one you should pursue. While I was ChristoPagan, I applied the version that included both Hekate and Jesus. When my beliefs changed, I applied this latter, Christian-specific form instead. If I had created the SSP earlier in my spiritual journey, the Hekate-specific form would have been my ideal. Again, this is a self-help system, and healing is the end goal. One only must be honest with oneself as to which version would work best for them. Being that we're trying to cultivate self-honesty, that is a proper and fitting first step. In the following chapter, we will discuss it in more detail.

Chapter XI:

Some Final Thoughts on Self-Honesty

To know oneself. To know your purpose. To be doing what you're born to do. These are lofty goals, but ones we all are searching for answers to. We are inundated with ideas of who and what we should be from the media, school, our families, friends, etc. But to find the answers to these questions, we must clear out the superfluous and go within.

This is the ultimate purpose of the Savior/Shadow Principle: as a potential facilitator to becoming self-compassionate through emulating compassionate archetypes, which could thereby create an inner atmosphere allowing us to work through self-deception and various outer noises to reach greater heights of self-honesty. That could ultimately allow us to grow and improve our quality of life. When we are honest with ourselves, we can make choices that will maximize our happiness; not fulfilling the well-meaning wishes of a parent, what we think society would approve of us being, etc., which may be contrary to what we truly desire. However, we must be able to practice self-honesty to find what we really want versus what we do out of needing acceptance, wanting to achieve notoriety, etc.

Once you have identified areas you need or want to work on, what career would be most satisfying to you, or other similar quality-of-life matters, now is the time to engage with these issues and continue your journey. As I shared earlier, after I received insight from the SSP, I found tangible ways to integrate that knowledge into my life. I didn't necessarily do those things right away, but I did ultimately take actionable steps. I was just at a point in life where I was ready to make big changes, so I had the willingness to move forward. Depending on your situation(s), you may need additional time to incorporate changes, allow for deep thought and reflection, evaluate different possibilities, etc.

Again, this is not a "one-time use" technique. For example, you may use the Savior/Shadow Principle to improve yourself as a single person, which allows you to be a more attractive relationship candidate. Because of this newfound attractiveness, you meet a partner and get married. This is now a new growth situation in which both you and your spouse will learn more about each other and yourselves. Again, the SSP can be re-used as the need arises.

As I said earlier, this is not a substitute for meeting with a mental health professional. This is merely a self-help technique; sometimes, we need to talk to them to get on the right track. There is nothing wrong with talking to someone;

I have myself! There are many reasons to visit a mental health professional: to use the above example again, a couple may need to visit a marriage counselor to strengthen their relationship. Per career, one may have to visit a career counselor to aid in narrowing down fields of interest. Sometimes, we can recognize a pattern of behaviors that aren't useful to us, and we require help in working through them. While we can make changes in our lives, sometimes additional assistance is necessary, and that's fine! Finally, recognizing that you need help is an exercise in self-honesty in and of itself...as well as self-compassion!

Now that we understand the SSP and how we can apply it to our daily lives, we must recognize that we ultimately strive for a happier, healthier life. We must be honest with ourselves—through the good, the bad, and the ugly, in order to access the reality of who we are. That's how we can identify the best way forward. The Savior/Shadow Principle could be beneficial in giving a framework to do just that.

Chapter XII:

Rounding Out the SSP

As we all know, it is hard to change. It can be uncomfortable and flat-out painful to see oneself objectively, flaws and all. However, achieving greater levels of personal growth, self-respect, confidence, and improved relationships with others requires self-reflection. To do so is to take the first steps into your shadow, inward Underworld or Sheol—which can be a harrowing task.

This is why having Hekate or Jesus (rather, imagining the archetypal energies they represent), per their stories we discussed, accompany you to these "dark places" can be helpful; they are representations of kindness towards yourself that may assist you with difficult inner work. This can be useful in getting to the truth: the truth of who you are, the truth of what you love, the reality of the person you are in totality.

Getting to the heart of your truth not only improves yourself but also those around you. When you are mentally and emotionally healthy, living your life in truth and acceptance of yourself, you are like a beacon of light shining brightly into the world. Seeing you living life fully, inspires others to do the same. If more of us live in full acceptance of ourselves, confidently and truthfully, this helps improve the world—one person at a time. Look at this book as an example: I went through difficulties, was honest with myself about what I was interested in, researched those things, and then found materials that aided my growth as a person. It facilitated finding authors of like mind that caused me to feel a level of acceptance I hadn't experienced before; my journey ultimately led me to develop the Savior/Shadow Principle. I have then continued with self-honesty and action and have achieved things that are true to the life I want to live. This technique and philosophy have been helpful to me and could be to others as well.

Finally, as this text is based upon honesty, I thought ending with a poem I authored would be particularly fitting. As I said earlier, in this journey of finding the true me, I have realized my love for writing poetry. I was inspired by all the works I have read along my journey, in addition to the SSP, to write the following poem, and I felt it was an appropriate end to this book. I hope you enjoy it, friend:

Become Your Hero

You can be

your life's greatest hero.
You can ascend
courageous,
renewed,
victorious,
into the rarefied air
of the heavens.
You can be
your life's greatest hero.
But you must first
conquer the depths,
you must slay the beasts
to discover the jewels.
They hide in the darkness.
It is treacherous work;
no lighthearted task is this!
But you, yes you,
have the strength within.
You can rise victorious!
Within you,
a warrior awaits to be released!

You can be

your life's greatest hero.

Be kind and truthful with yourself,

conquer your "depths,"

and become your life's greatest hero!

Or in SSP-specific language:

Delve into your Shadow

in order to become your own Savior!

Works Cited

Campbell, Joseph. *The Hero with a Thousand Faces*. 3rd ed., New World Library, 2008.

d'Este, Sorita. *Hekate Liminal Rites: A Study of the Rituals, Magic and Symbols of the Torch-bearing Triple Goddess of the Crossroads*. Avalonia, 2009.

Dillon, John. *The Middle Platonists: 80 B.C. to A.D. 220*. Cornell University Press, 1977.

Higginbotham, Joyce and River Higginbotham. *ChristoPaganism: An Inclusive Path*. Llewellyn Publications, 2009.

"Hymn 2 to Demeter." *The Homeric Hymns and Homerica*. Translated by Hugh G. Evelyn-White, Harvard University Press; William Heinemann Ltd., 1914. *Tufts University - Perseus Digital Library*, http://data.perseus.org/citations/urn:cts:greekLit:tlg0013.tlg002.perseus-eng1:2. Accessed 3 May 2024.

Johnston, Sarah Iles. *Hekate Soteira: A Study of Hekate's Roles in the Chaldean Oracles and Related Literature*. Scholars Press, 1990.

Jung, Carl G. *Aion: Researches into the Phenomenology of the Self*. 2nd ed. Translated by R. F. C. Hull, Princeton University Press, 1969.

---. *The Archetypes and the Collective Unconscious*. 2nd ed. Translated by R. F. C. Hull, Princeton University Press, 1969.

McAfee, Kimberly. "Additional Thoughts on the Savior/Shadow Principle with Christo-Pagan Original Draft." *Academia*, 2018, https://www.academia.edu/37580054/Additional_Thoughts_on_the_Savior_Shadow_Principle_with_Christo_Pagan_Original_Draft. Accessed 12 July 2019.

---. "...And Those Reborn." *Of Imagination and Daydreams*. *Channillo*, 17 November 2019, https://channillo.com/series/of-imagination-and-daydreams/. Accessed 15 January 2020.

---. "Not Just a Necklace: Using Pendants as a Self-Help Tool to Alleviate Anxiety." *Academia*, 2018, https://www.academia.edu/36386745/NOT_JUST_A_NECKLACE_USING_PENDANTS_AS_A_SELF_HELP_TOOL_TO_ALLEVIATE_ANXIETY. Accessed 23 August 2019.

---. "Of Perished Dreams..." *Of Imagination and Daydreams*. *Channillo*, 17 November 2019, https://channillo.com/series/of-imagination-and-daydreams/. Accessed 15 January 2020.

---. "The Savior/Shadow Principle: The Post-Crucifixion Experience of Jesus Christ as an Archetypal Blueprint for Personal Growth." *Academia*, 2018, https://www.academia.edu/36387329/THE_SAVIOR_SHADOW_PRINCIPLE_THE_POST_CRUCIFIXION_EXPERIENCE_OF_JESUS_CHRIST_AS_AN_ARCHETYPAL_BLUEPRINT_FOR_PERSONAL_GROWTH. Accessed 12 July 2019.

---. "Thoughts of Grace." *No Love Truer: A Chapbook of Christian Poetry*. *Channillo*, 25 September 2020, https://channillo.com/series/no-love-truer-a-chapbook-of-christian-poetry/. Accessed 1 October 2020.

Ovid. "Daphne and Phoebus—lines 452-524." *Metamorphoses*. Translated by Brookes More, Cornhill Publishing Co., 1922. *Tufts University - Perseus Digital Library*, http://data.perseus.org/citations/urn:cts:latinLit:phi0959.phi006.perseus-eng1:1.452-1.524. Accessed 7 June 2024.

---. "Daphne and Phoebus—lines 525-566." Metamorphoses. Translated by Brookes More, Cornhill Publishing Co., 1922. *Tufts University - Perseus Digital Library*, http://data.perseus.org/citations/urn:cts:latinLit:phi0959.phi006.perseus-eng1:1.525-1.566. Accessed 7 June 2024.

St. Clair, Adelina. *The Path of a Christian Witch*. Llewellyn Publications, 2009.

Townsend, Mark. *Jesus through Pagan Eyes: Bridging Neopagan Perspectives with a Progressive Vision of Christ*. Llewellyn Publications, 2012.

***For additional information on the goddess Amaterasu:
https://www.britannica.com/topic/Amaterasu

***For additional information on the #WeStandWithU event by Poetizer:
https://poetizer.com/initiatives/we-stand-with-u

Appendix A

The following poems were written during my mid-life crisis mentioned in the "My Personal Story" section; I believe they accurately portray what I was experiencing, which was pertinent to beginning my journey into alternative spirituality. I wanted to share with you the great pressure of my emotions at that time (to use imagery from the Savior/Shadow Principle, I was embarking on a trip to my inner Underworld or inner Sheol), and I feel that where my factual relaying of the past may fail, the art I created then makes up for that. The first is a bit somber but very accurate to what I felt. The second is more aspirational; I was still battling with acceptance but was hopeful. I recognized I needed to make more realistic, unique-to-me goals (the self-honesty I gained is on display here) to improve my life, like writing this very book. It is my sincerest hope that you enjoy them:

Of Perished Dreams...

This graveyard of dead dreams
I am surrounded
By decaying possibilities
Of what I could have been
Of where I could have gone
Of who I could have known
Some I now know needed to die
They don't fit who I have become
Some I can barely look at
Even in their rotting states
They hold a glimmer
A sparkle
That is painful to ignore
But alas, they cannot be revived

Life has grown in ways that make them impossible to realize
Sometimes pretty dreams need to die
To make room for beautiful realities
A land of melancholy
A place we all visit
A place we must accept
A place we must reconcile (McAfee, "Of Perished Dreams...")

...And Those Reborn

From the ashes of perished dreams
Mixed with sobering tears
And soul-crushing heartbreak
Are new dreams birthed
Reborn
From the carcasses of their ancestors
Refined
Made stronger, made smarter
Rarefied
Uniquely mine, a result of all my
previous experiences
Realistic
No more child-like fantasies
But reliant on my true strengths
I am now stronger
I am now much happier
I am now whole (McAfee, "...And Those
Reborn")

Appendix B

Similar to the previous Appendix, I wrote the following poem during the time described in the "My Current Path" section; I felt overtaken by the idea of grace. I share this not to proselytize but to show the magnitude of my feelings at the time—that I was so moved by it that I created art. These thoughts gave me pause, and I pondered my life in general: my loved ones, my purpose, the meaning of life, my triumphs and errors (admittedly, I was focused more on the latter than the former, so grace was particularly appealing), everything. I returned to Christianity at this time. The following poem is an excerpt from my chapbook, *No Love Truer:*

A Chapbook of Christian Poetry, on Amazon.com; it captures the emotions I had then completely, which were all stepping stones on my spiritual journey and for writing this book. For those interested, the poems in this chapbook are traditionally Christian. Again, I hope you enjoy it:

Thoughts of Grace

Thoughts of grace consume me
How could have I been so blind?
A gift I took for granted
I now run to, with arms wide open

I have sinned so many times before
Made so many mistakes
But You, the God of All
Forgive me completely

I can barely fathom Your love
To have Your Beloved Son die for our
sins

My sins
All washed away by His Blood

How the God Who created all
The universe, the planets
The mountains, the trees
The sky and the seas

Could care so much for me
For each and every one of us
All humankind for all of time
Completely astonishes me

Thank you, Heavenly Father
For these gifts You have given us
For Your unending love
I am brought to tears by Your mercy

Thoughts of grace consume me
Finally, I understand
Your gifts to us all, so plentiful
I now accept them, with heart wide open
(McAfee, "Thoughts of Grace").

Special Thanks

First, I want to thank my family and particularly, my dad. Thank you all for your continuous love and support; I appreciate you all more than words can say! For my father, David: thank you so much for your encouragement. You helped me gain the confidence to write this book, which means so much to me! Dads really do know best!

Big thanks to Stephanie Lamb, Dylan Webster, and the Quillkeepers Press, LLC team (@quillkeeperspress on Instagram)! Thank you so much for publishing this book; it is precious to me, and I'm very grateful that you have helped me share it with the world. You all are awesome and highly appreciated!

Special thanks to Sorita d'Este (https://www.soritadeste.com). She is an amazing researcher and writer, and her work has been a big part of my journey. I am delighted to have been able to share some of her writings through this text; it is definitely a full circle moment for me! Thank you for all that you do!

I also want to thank all the people who shared books, information, encouragement, friendship, etc., while I was a practicing ChristoPagan. I have lost touch with them over time; some of them, I never even knew their real names! But wherever you are, I appreciate your kindness while I was learning. Many thanks to you!

Also, big thanks to the beautiful souls who are part of the poetry community on Instagram! Thank you for the friendship, encouragement, and kindness you have shared with me. You all have brought me tons of joy, and I'm looking forward to what the future holds for all of us!

Lastly, thank you for reading this book! As I said earlier, I consider this my magnum opus, so I feel anyone who reads this has shared a very special experience with me. I hope it proves helpful to you and inspires you to learn and grow. You are a special and unique person with special and unique contributions to this world. Thank you again for sharing this experience with me!

About the Author

Kimberly McAfee is a writer and poet residing in the US. She has authored/co-authored works in a variety of formats, such as websites, e-magazines, anthologies, and even a peer-reviewed scholarly journal. Ms. McAfee has published the poetry collection, *The Savior and the Shadow Queen: A Fantastical Tale Told Through Sequential Poems,* and the chapbook, *AmerAsian: My Journey to Becoming Whole as a Mixed Korean-American,* with Quillkeepers Press. She has also self-published three chapbooks, *Consumed: A Collection of Poems for the Modern Romantic*, *The Siren's Call: A Horror and Halloween Themed Poetry Collection*, and *No Love Truer: A Chapbook of Christian*

Poetry, which are available on Amazon. You can find more of her poetry on her Instagram page @writerpoetkim.

For more information about Joseph Campbell,
please visit the Joseph Campbell Foundation at
JCF.org.

What Others Are Saying about
The Savior/Shadow Principle

The Savior/Shadow Principle by Kimberly McAfee is a deeply inspiring self-help book that blends academic insight with the transformative power of guided meditation. Drawing from a wealth of knowledge and experience, McAfee explores the hidden aspects of ourselves that must be acknowledged to cultivate a more authentic and fulfilling life. Thought-provoking and introspective, this book is a must-read for anyone seeking to deepen their spirituality and embark on a journey of self-discovery.

—Serena Morrigan
Author of *Tea for the Wicked* & *A Song for Every Scar*

The Savior/Shadow Principle provides a broad perspective of faiths and spiritual beliefs. Merging these and reflecting on similarities can serve as a model for your life direction. Definition and application examples are provided that are simple, yet expandable to anyone's situation. Most important, are Kimberly's meaningful successes derived from the information presented in this book. Everyone stumbles as we travel down the road of life, and the processes discussed could be helpful on that journey. We all love and are Extremely Proud of Kimberly!

—David McAfee
Kimberly's Father

Kimberly McAfee's *The Savior/Shadow Principle* (SSP) is a unique blend of mythology, spirituality, and self-help. It uses archetypes to guide personal transformation. Drawing from her experiences with Christianity, ChristoPaganism, and alternative spiritual paths, McAfee develops a technique to foster self-honesty, growth, and healing.

Summary:
At its core, SSP is a meditation-based self-help method that utilizes the figures of Hekate, a complex goddess from ancient traditions, and Jesus, the central figure of Christianity, as archetypal guides. The book explores duality, mythological parallels, and psychological integration, encouraging self-reflection and personal

evolution. McAfee thoroughly examines both deities, their historical significance, and their symbolic meanings before introducing her structured meditation practice, which involves introspective "journeys" with Hekate and Jesus.

Kimberly frames the book as a culmination of her personal spiritual evolution, transitioning from Christianity to ChristoPaganism and then to a non-traditional form of Christianity. She emphasizes the importance of self-honesty, allowing individuals to examine their personal truths, shadow aspects, and inner conflicts through a compassionate lens. The method encourages users to metaphorically "descend" into their subconscious (shadow work) with Hekate's guidance and then "ascend" with Jesus, fostering self-awareness and transformation.

Key Points:
1. Innovative Approach to Self-Help
Integrating archetypal mythology with meditation-based introspection is a refreshing take on self-help. By blending psychological and spiritual elements, SSP offers a versatile tool for those interested in alternative methods of self-discovery.

2. Deeply Personal and Relatable

Kimberly shares her own journey with raw honesty, making the book engaging and relatable. Her willingness to explore her past experiences adds depth and authenticity.

3. Well-researched and Thoughtful

The book provides historical and mythological context, making it informative for readers unfamiliar with Hekate, ChristoPaganism, or Jungian archetypes.

4. Encourages Open-Minded Exploration

Kimberly does not impose a single belief system but encourages readers to use SSP as a flexible tool adaptable to various spiritual perspectives.

Final Thoughts:

"The Savior/Shadow Principle" is a thought-provoking and introspective read for those open to blending spiritual archetypes with personal growth techniques. Its unique fusion of mythology, psychology, and self-help makes it stand out in the genre, particularly for those interested in mythological archetypes, personal transformation, and open-minded spiritual exploration. Readers seeking a fresh perspective on self-reflection and healing may find this book valuable.

—Kim V. Poetry
Author of *Remember Me* and *Heartbreaks at 3 a.m.*